Also by Michael Meyerhofer

BOOKS

Blue Collar Eulogies. Steel Toe Books
Leaving Iowa. Briery Creek Press

CHAPBOOKS

Pure Elysium. Palettes and Quills
Real Courage. Jeanne Duval Editions
The Clay-Shaper's Husband. Codhill Press
The Right Madness of Beggars. Uccelli Press
Cardboard Urn. Southeast Missouri State University Press

DAMNATIO MEMORIAE

DAMNATIO MEMORIAE

Winner of the Brick Road Poetry Prize

Poems by Michael Meyerhofer

BRICK ROAD

POETRY PRESS

Special thanks to
Mary Biddinger, Djelloul Marbrook, Barbara Ungar,
Alysha Hoffa, Peter Davis, Ron Self,
Keith Badowski, Anne Ulanov, Steven Shields,
Donna Marbach, Tom Holmes, Jared Sexton,
Todd McKinney, C.J. Sage and Dorianne Laux

CONTENTS

I. *Flowstones*

II. *Stalagmites*

III. *The Undirected Object*

IV. *Divine Prepositions*

Introduction

Like most publishers, we at Brick Road Poetry Press list submission guidelines on our website. Additionally we go beyond the guidelines to include lists of "characteristics we like" and "characteristics we dislike." In *Damnatio Memoriae*, the winner of the Brick Road Poetry Prize, Michael Meyerhofer gives the impression of having gone down that list to check off each item one by one with almost every poem in the collection.

As to the characteristics we dislike, he avoids them all, including no "intentional obscurity or riddling," no "highfalutin vocabulary" or "lack of recognizable theme or topic." Without a doubt, these poems reveal wise insights on the human perspective, but never at the cost of being overly serious, scholarly, or mysterious. The reader of these poems faces no risk of boredom—quite the contrary.

Imagination and a beguiling tongue-in-cheek tone are the trademarks of Michael Meyerhofer's poetry. His work hits all our "like" buttons as it speaks in "a coherent human voice," though not always his own or the one you might expect, but one with "a sense of humor" that uses "words and language as [a] springboard for playful exploration."

In many of these poems, the speaker possesses an inquisitive mind with an avid interest in history and even pre-history, fueled by the Discovery and History channels, Google searches, and museums. These poems dramatize a mind capable of straddling centuries, combining in the same breath an ancient scene with a contemporary evaluation, as when in the title poem, "Damnatio Memoriae," we encounter a Roman "slave/who fell from a twine-wrapped ladder/that OSHA would never condone." Such use of anachronism strikes us as both clever and funny.

In "The Original Swastika," we're guided briskly through history, spotting the association-laden symbol in cultures as varied as the Romans, early Christians, Buddhists, Hindus, Navajos, and finally, "on the hoods /of German sedans." This whirlwind tour succinctly reminds us that the meanings of symbols morph over time and across cultures and that our recent memories and associations tend to obscure the resonances assigned in prior eras.

His persona poems conjure speakers from worlds we know and from worlds we wish we knew, and every scene, setting or experience is depicted intensely with concrete imagery and drama. At first blush, "Dear Students," appears to argue for the conceit that writing poetry today rises from the same impulse that produced Stone Age cave paintings. Yet the poem does so much more than simply propose a comparison. It actually delivers a vivid experience from the point of view of a Paleolithic hunter, as if to say poetry is about beauty, guilt, and survival.

Although many of these poems pursue history, the contemporary perspective and the everyday moment are not neglected. In "For Tanya, Whose Fate Remains Unknown," the speaker receives a phone call about "bad news" concerning a daughter he doesn't have. The surprise of the erroneous call sets off a poignant daydream of what peril the "daughter" Tanya might be suffering, and then an even deeper imagining of memories that might be slipping away from Tanya as she bleeds.

These poems wake you up with their surprising twists, with the intensity of their speakers, and with the inventiveness of their lines and concepts. Sometimes these poems even risk offending the reader by tampering with archetypes, as in "Hansel's Redemption" where the question of what ever happened to Hansel and Gretel is answered with a scandalous narrative.

As you may have guessed, *Damnatio Memoriae* easily asserted itself as the winner of our inaugural Brick Road Poetry Prize. Given the liveliness of Meyerhofer's poetry, this introduction is, in comparison, the only potentially tedious moment of the entire book. We're proud to be publishing it and further encourage you to seek out Michael Meyerhofer's other books immediately.

Keith Badowski & Ron Self, Editors
Brick Road Poetry Press
Columbus, GA

And we are magic talking to itself,
noisy and alone.

—Anne Sexton

I

Flowstones

Damnatio Memoriae

How much cleaner was the sky
before the last laughing owl
turned up slap-stiff in New Zealand,
alongside words like *leeftail*
which meant *to be in great demand,*
an irony lost on the last dinosaur
who tried in vain to drink
from a steaming lake, teeth
weeping into its own reflection.
If suffering breeds wisdom,
might we have found salvation
in a lost syllable of Kwadi,
the exhale of that last cry pansy,
the last Roman surgeon
to use a bone lever on a slave
who fell from a twine-wrapped ladder
that OSHA would never condone?
I want to believe we are all
just rough drafts of the same assignment,
a holy exercise in translation.
I want to believe in the grace
of the last person to use a cecograph—
which I just read was a device
to help blind people write,
rendered obsolete by what now
yields nothing but spam porn
when I search for images of *cecograph,*
its face lost like the dear papyrus
torn from the only copies of Sappho,

the Nag Hammadi scrolls
accidentally burned by farmers
who needed warmth, after all,
more than that 1787 Chateau Lafite
bottled by Thomas Jefferson
(spoiled when lamp-heat melted the cork)
or one's chances to saddle
eohippus, the dawn horse,
smaller than a wild dog.
Meaning we would have to be
smaller still than those Palau pygmies
who surrendered size for spears
as lack of food shrank
their brains, the same way
hunger shrank the gray muscles
of all those elephants who died
with tusks barely matching
the height of lions' teeth.
Going back to Rome, it's said
that the names of let-downs
could be struck from remembrance,
no busts or faces on coins,
not even a mention at family
reunions over bowls of figs and oil,
all they'd done simply
forgotten, like the use of *yelve*—
those dung-forks used for centuries
to facilitate regrowth,
dark waste yielding plants
with lungfuls of water and light.

Skandha

You nurse the origami of your theory
that we are all the same person,
born from stencils but with different scars,

creases in the palimpsests of water.
Then you read how electrons
with their sour habit of disappearing

like teens out bedroom windows
then slipping back in well after curfew
with those shy, tight smiles

point to the existence of other realities,
hiccups in one's love for sushi
or willingness to wear small animals.

Elsewhere, another kind of me
drinks puréed fiber and votes Republican
while a yesteryou folds lingerie

with plastic chopsticks in your hair.
I imagine time as a school bus
painted the wrong color,

that you are the one with a box turtle
asleep in a nest of newspaper, that I am still
haggling over football cards

with other farm boys in love
with their own biceps, fists a kind of mudra,
shame a kind of loam in our blood.

The Revision

I decided to take your advice
on my poem. The penultimate stanza
has been shifted to the end.
I now describe the Jehovah's Witness
using third-person omniscient.
You were right, by the way,
about my reference to Theodote,
not to mention that line
about eating a plate of hot wings
just to try and feel something.
Yes, Iowa really does have dogwoods.
Yes, Yo-Yo Ma really forgot
his own cello in a Manhattan cab.
But I meant it as a compliment
when I called you ergonomic.
No, you're right about me
needing to think less about circumcision
and more about white dwarf stars,
which are really just diamonds
ringing like Tibetan gongs in the deep.
Even so, I want to tell you
about the hiccup in my aorta
when you stretched tonight, your thumb
between stanzas, nose-ring
catching the moon… well, *just so*.

Father Time and Baby New Year

There he goes, toddling off-stage
with that gnarled scythe resting
crosswise a sash in last year's fashion,
his dripstone beard, his great
nose like a pilgrim's plough-blade.

And here comes his successor—
a drooling infant dressed in a top hat
and star-spangled diaper,
blissfully unaware how he will age
three months each day in office.

Father Time could say something.
He could warn the poor toddler
of the need to arm himself,
to get a handle on more than his bowels
if he wants to hold this mess together.

But Baby New Year just grins
like a pacifist and the old man departs,
yielding at last his gothic hourglass
of sand made from the bones
of dinosaurs, sea cows, Babylonians—

all that expires under Time's watch.
Meanwhile, the Dutch launch fireworks,
the Greeks bake coins in cakes,
Japanese monks ring temple bells
and the Scots gift coal and shortbread.

But here, we Americans just kiss
and kiss while that old drama plays out
on confetti-fogged billboards,
the tips of noisemakers blaring up one
strangled, universal note to the sky.

Lament For the Pilgrims of Qin Shi Huang

In the inevitable twilight of his reign,
after burning books and Confucians
to further the vanity of his unified China,
while his artisans were busy
chiseling the terracotta warriors—
clay men dressed better than they were—
a rumor spread across the countryside
of mushroom-shaped islands
where immortals lived, brewing elixirs
to stave off their own recycling.

But of course, such things require
a sacrifice, so the emperor sent hundreds
of young people on ships
laden with supplies and treasure.
Imagine trying to keep a straight face
as you sail out of the harbor,
on your way to make a new life
well beyond the emperor's steely reach.
Or maybe you wept to leave
families you could never see again.

Legend says that Japan was founded
by these pilgrims who knew better
than to sail back to China empty-handed.
Isn't that always the way of it?
Some bloated fool in purple silk orders you
to fetch grace he has not earned.
But before you find it—if you ever do—
you have to cling pitifully to a vessel
packed with swords, heaving east
beneath the bone-white wheels of heaven.

The Birthdays of Ex-Lovers

How they pinball through the mind
like the combinations of outgrown lockers,
a mishmash of Virgos and Cancers

on whose soft favor we once depended—
useless now like the few syllables
bored in from foreign language classes,

the equations of elementary physics
they swore we must memorize
if we held any hope for future happiness.

But no—the world knuckles along
whether we remember or not,
hauling everyone for whom the heart once

flounced like a broadsided schooner,
for whom we raised mythologies
all sin-sweet, proud as a dead religion.

Muskoxen

Like wooly frigates they drift—
(great(horned)druids) of the Canadian Arctic.
When threatened
                they form up:

an even greater circle
the calves inside
all the calves nuzzled safely in

while the bulls and cows
male and female
alike

stare out—placid as a lake
on fire—until danger
gives up
       , slumps off.   There is nothing

quite so lone-
some as hunger.

To the President of the American Begonia Society

Although we've never met, I think it's great you love begonias
enough to run for president of the American Begonia Society—

if that's how you got the gig, not a *coup d'état* against Janet B.,
former president, shown in photos handing a trophy to some chap

from the Scottish Begonia Society, with whom I imagine a rivalry
of which exists no proof. Just think—the Great Depression

was all it took for Long Beach horticulturists to get together
and coin the society motto: *Stimulating begonia interest since 1932.*

Surely, this beats my motto: *Sweeping the leg since 1977,*
an obscure reference to that classic 80s film, *The Karate Kid*—

implausible, too, since I was not the most agile of infants
and not quite up to martial arts. But I digress. It would seem

you have fifty-four branches around the country, meaning I
or someone I know probably knows someone who drove past

on the way to some begonialess job, felt oddly hollow, and didn't
know why. Now, I know. Moving along. I looked you up

because my goddaughter just showed me her favorite photo:
a cream-colored begonia with orange fringe, species unknown

or at least not stated in the caption. I know you are the one
to contact about this. I have in mind a trade. Please ask

any questions you have about print journals versus ezines,
how to do proper MLA citation, where to buy a blowgun.

I also make a mean beef stew, but I imagine that's no big deal
to a woman out to *standardize the nomenclature of begonias*

and promote other *shade-loving plants*. I find it entirely possible—
at least, I want to find it entirely possible—that poets

are shade-loving plants who accidentally learned to talk.
In that case, Mary S., you may know me better than anyone.

The Original Swastika

Look for it on Thor's hammer,
shards of Greek pottery, silk tapestries
from old China. Whittled by Ukrainians
in spans of mammoth bone, sewn
into the feathered gowns of Quetzalcóatl.
Raised rune over the Buddha's heart.
Crest of the early Christians
who borrowed from the very Romans
they were hiding from, long after
its axles and rays symbolized rebirth
in the belly of a Trojan goddess.
In Hinduism, marking thresholds and doors.
A Navajo prayer for good fortune,
a metaphor balancing mountains and rain.
Sometimes backwards, sometimes not.
Sometimes, the arms are replaced
with a woman's blowing hair.
Sometimes the tips end in playful swirls
to symbolize migration. Luck
tattooed in lime, scattered
on the pewter coins of Gaul.
Ages before the cross or the ankh,
before black snow piled on the hoods
of German sedans, this one symbol
spread across oceans. A genetic dream.
Our birthright, our redemption—fueling
the pyres of all we've already lost.

Dear Students,

Know this: there is nothing more
Paleolithic than writing poetry.

The ballpoints you bought, five
for a dollar, are the grandchildren

of ash-chalk and animal blood
painted by geniuses on cave walls,

painted by wild-haired hunters
who lived off charred meat

ripped right from the bone by
the same fists that drove the spears,

the spears tipped in knapped flint
five hundred times sharper

than the best surgeon's scalpel.
True, you could fuss with oil paints

or pirouette to *The Nutcracker,*
but these will get you no further

than what it took to describe,
before the holy advent of gerunds,

before Man's exodus from dripstone,
your beloved half-shadowed by fire.

The swath of the beast's antlers.
How it lowered its freckled snout

to the stream. Those umber hooves.
The guilt before the spear-throw.

The World's Oldest Dildo

Long before the Shroud of Turin
or an Antikythera Mechanism
drawn up swamped with sea-rust,

nearly three hundred centuries
before Tutankhamun's death mask,
this polished siltstone relic

found its way into a German cave.
Sure, it's worth a snicker, imagining
Ice Age couples with sex toys,

but still it strikes me as quaint—
hunched shoulders carefully sanding
out every potential snag, a mate

smirking across the campfire,
a hide hung over the cave-mouth.
How to know that the wind outside

would go on howling that way,
so many ages of chariots and gore?
That the stars were just stars,

that no gods hurled the lightning
or left berries under the ice?
Let's give it a test run, one of them said

in a series of Ice Age grunts,
and through no miracle but their own,
they crafted heat to melt the glaciers.

Wisdom of the Ancients

My friend tells me this story:
how, before he and his wife married,
merely living in sin, his father
questioned her wisdom by asking
Why buy the cow when
you can get the milk for free?
And for the rest of the afternoon,
I can't help but apply this
logic to other scenarios—say,
my class attendance policy
when I'll gladly email the notes
to any student willing
to not give me a bad evaluation.
The fact I'm working at all
when welfare alone might keep me
stocked in caffeine and ink.
So too all those women for whom
I've written love poems
even though they weren't interested
in anything but love poems.
They say that ancient Romans
used to rip out the flooring
of their coliseum and flood it,
i.e., why go to sea when you can see
a naval battle right here?
Imagine sitting with your kids,
munching a snack, watching
condemned men splash and drown.
Finally, the kids stop crying

about their mother's typhoid.
The youngest points and laughs,
the sound pure Elysium over the din,
and you remember why
you had them in the first place.

Ode to Coprolite

Over fourteen thousand years ago,
a Siberian who followed the snowy herds
all the way to Oregon
squatted in a cave and had
no idea that archeologists with calipers
and white beards would puzzle
over the remnants of his
charred dinner, extrapolate his whole
life from the unexpectedly lovely
spirals of a fossilized turd.

Now I wonder what will happen
a few dozen centuries from now
when they crack open the sewers and discover
my aversion to vegetables,
my fondness for Belgian ale,
my ancestors who must have followed
a knot of McDonalds all the way
from Czechoslovakia to Indianapolis.

Shame that we cannot be judged
for more than what we leave behind:
rust layered under ice,
forests brambled with ash.
And all those take-out boxes
decorated with clowns and gymnasts,
not to honor the gods
but to catch the eye before
we tossed them out the window.

Ode to Raccoons

When you asked what raccoons eat,
I said, *Anything, they'll literally eat anything.*
You went on fixing your poem
and didn't even chide me for being
probably the ten thousandth person that day
to misuse the word, *literally.*
As though I might go out to the garage
this morning and find that raccoons
have gotten in my barrel of carburetors again,
gnawing on last summer's ruddy nails,
feasting on liver-shaped shards
of busted sidewalk. How to be angry, though,
at a creature who can live off sand and pantyhose,
who metabolizes wine corks and converts
the sticks left over from corndogs
into mother's milk for a whole new gaze of raccoons?
See how they chew through the national debt,
how they make tea from our bad dreams,
how even prejudice tastes to them
like salmon in ginger sauce. No wonder
they sometimes go mad, weighed down as they are
by so much undigested scorn,
unfathomable ounces of heartache.
No wonder even the saints among us
reach for pellet guns whenever they show up,
claws poised, ready to rip open
trash bags filled with human regret
that, to a raccoon, must smell like paradise.

Why Girls Walk Home

—A Hollywood short film from 1929

So these four flappers get a flat tire
next to the beach—what to do
but shrug off a few pounds of cloth and go

skinny-dipping—which, in 1929,
means splashing about in underwear
layered like a nun's habit.

Then this little black girl
in a sail-white bonnet, peering out
from a few shy fingers of rock,

steals their clothes—then, it seems,
their car. The women don't care.
They just laugh, hook arms and high-step

into the celluloid archives
of my great-grandfather's time.
But the girl, that little savant with a jack

who could change a flat tire
that left four white women all thumbs—
I imagine her driving off

into some black and white sunset,
feet barely reaching the pedals,
content to enjoy her trophies off-camera.

The Secret Lives of Rocket Scientists

Looks like we've still got them fooled!
they joke, quitting early and heading for the bar.
The boss—the only one wearing
a jacket and tie—changes in the van,
laughing and toking off the communal joint
as he buttons up his Hawaiian shirt
halfway. *What's so damn hard about this?*
Gary asks, waving the stack of theorems
on fluid mechanics that they use
for deseeding. Phil shrugs. He talks about
how his dad spent a Saturnian orbit
at the brickyard, palms raw as a heart attack.
Cheryl chimes in—her great-aunt's
arthritic fingers still wrap cheeseburgers
while a pimply manager takes shots
of girls' asses with his cell phone.
Next comes Barry's brother-in-law,
the cautionary tale of his doctorate in ceramics.
A solemn hush falls over the van. By now
they're parked, red bar signs flashing
through smoke-washed windows.
When the lull gets to be like dark matter,
Ahmed asks which Ramsay discovered neon.
They all answer at once. The boss
takes off his horn-rimmed glasses, rubs his eyes,
slides the frames into his shirt pocket.
Hours later they're still orbiting the waitress,
wiping their mouths with pulsar-white napkins.
Then Chuck compares Barry's wife
to Valles Marineris, and they erupt in guffaws

so great the bartender asks them to leave.
Hey, you deadbeats, get a real job!
he calls after them, sweeping up
the doodled equations, the fake phone numbers,
that starry mess of busted shot glasses.

Physicist's Love Letter

I ought to be more clear
when I say that I miss your touch.
After all, it's just the fields
around your electrons scooting mine
to one side. Put another way,
how my parts reshuffle
whenever yours draw close.

Post Grads

Like *rōnin* minus the fighting prowess
and sense of honor, they wander
along highways and neglected railroads,
from town to town in search
of health care and a 2/2 teaching load.

Often we spot them in gazebos,
near wild geese or some manmade lake,
in Irish pubs that act like pockets
of hippy dissent in otherwise
all-white, right-wing college towns.

Know them by their red flannels,
their careful bangs and uncrossed legs,
their knowledge of Belgian beer.
Theirs are the cars in the parking lot
most desperately in need of brake pads.

When pressures burst, they retire
to bookstores and coffee shops, egos
propped over steamed milk,
hoping the next thing they see won't be
a former student's name in print.

But always they are drawn back
to classrooms the size of their apartments,
lectures on the Deep Imagists,
the pitfalls of verb tense and how to
salvage these endings, these heroic failures.

Industrial Grade Diamonds

No one cares what color we are.
Dug up, we are prized for our hardness,
our knack for weathering the inferno.
We are nature's superheroes,
vanguards of drill bits and saws, our names
derived from *adámas*, Greek word
for *proper, untamed.* Down where rock
becomes water, deeper than worms,
only at the end do we see the sky.
Call this birth, call this death if you want.
When that blaze, unable to kill us,
spits us out instead. Or else
some fool with a shovel disturbs
our billion-year meditation.
Nowadays, they make us in labs,
proof monkeys *can* write Shakespeare.
We cause no friction when rubbed together,
though still we try. Some of us
got here on the red backs of asteroids.
Come so far, we spend the rest
of our lives trying to remember home.

Yggdrasil

It seems silly now—the idea
that all the world rests in the branches
of a colossal ash tree.
But maybe the Norse had it right,
whispering over campfires
and freshly honed axes.
These days, quantum physics
speaks of parallel universes,
cosmic soap bubbles
drifting through the bulk,
so why couldn't all the galaxies
be swirls in a turtle's shell,
dew off the tip of a broadleaf?
It might be nice to learn
that the world is flat after all,
that breaking a mirror somehow
incites photons against us,
that pregnant women with heartburn
really *are* more likely to bear
children with a full head of hair.
Believe, just for a moment,
in the benevolence of the wishbone.
That we are held aloft
by the palms of a great tree
born in ages past from an acorn
no bigger than a singularity.

Ode to the Boxing Clapboard

Fifty thousand crowd Cowboys Stadium tonight.
After the Filipino National Anthem sung by the new
lead singer of Journey, after the Star-Spangled Banner
sung by three prim cheerleaders in shorts
borrowed from their baby sisters, after Pacquiao
pummels Clottey's forearms until veins
ripple like sand dunes, tail-end of each round,
the Timekeeper rises in his spiffy tuxedo, braces himself
and works the hinge twice—ten seconds left,
wooden clap deafening the grunts, blood tap-dancing
off eardrums. This is my favorite part of boxing:
this trinket pilfered from a movie set,
two spray-painted boards and a hinge from Home Depot.
Jumbo screens and million dollar contracts but this
is what they listen for—these men who do push-ups
by the thousands, these pot-bellied howlers
sloshing their overpriced beer. Even us poor writers
watching on pay-per-view, imagining over hot wings
all we could have done with an entourage
of cameras. How we might have made a living
off more than our sad sack brains, this backhanded
longing to applaud someone else's glory.

II

Stalagmites

Poem Written on the Second Sunday in May, Thirteen Years after My Mother's Death

Strange that I still remember the houseflies
roiling on the chipped windowsill of that shack

where we lived during the lonesome eternity
of my single digits. Most of the time,

I was filthy—still in diapers, unmedicated
for the crooked spine I was born with, unwashed

by a woman who tried sleeping off her
diabetes. A field of slack corn to the north,

ruddy glint of silo-caps punted by tornados,
the vegetable garden we planted but gave up on.

And the houseflies: fat as a toddler's knuckle,
banging their dark skulls on the window frame,

jostling the world with their needful hunger.
Still this, too, warrants mention—how first frost

glazed the intricacy of last night's cobwebs.
How the same winter that knotted our drains

left icicles like inverted battlements. How
twilight bred whole squadrons of dragonflies,

crows flying indifferent sorties overhead,
their aloofness anchoring my gaze to the sky.

Before Rilke Was a Man

I wanted Rilke to be a woman the first time I came
across his selected at a rummage sale, chancing upon

The Panther, ink prowling between taut margins.
It was summer break. I asked my mom to get it for me.

For two quarters, a better buy than those ratty
paperbacks of sword-wielding men and fawny maids

in chain mail who never held my attention for long.
I liked the idea of a woman who liked the idea

of panthers—besides, wasn't his middle name Maria?
How to know Rainer was German, not Cherokee?

I pictured her staking out zoos, feathers in her braids,
her soft eyes noting each shudder of captive grace.

In dreams she climbed a barbed fence to find me—
her foreign tongue, the flint knife hidden in her skirt.

Dear Brigitte Nielsen,

When Grandpa caught me watching *Red Sonja,*
all those Italian girls dressed in chain mail blouses

chopping at bad guys with rubber swords,
he was already drunk—it was Sunday, after all—

and since it takes almost nothing to enrage
a vet with untreated anxiety disorders, he went off

about how your place was in the kitchen,
not hacking down misunderstood monsters.

How women were made to care for men like him—
guys who marry women like my grandmother

who grew seven children in her private garden,
baby-sat me while my mother was on dialysis

and hardly ever interrupted her husband's tirades
after he threw a television through the window.

No wonder I dream so often of snapping
bullies over my knee like bloody twigs.

No wonder I fall for slash-and-dash heroines
armored against the charms of language.

Ode to that Woman in Hartford City, Indiana, Who Wanted Nothing to Do with Me

Rolling at sundown into Hartford City,
home to a bowling alley turned lesbian bar
turned bowling alley, where drafts
lean into the soft fists of retired coaches
feigning hope in tonight's big screen blow-out,
past nowhere then left on Kickapoo,
I find my friend's station wagon
parked over a crumpled moth of motor oil.
Thus resumes our yearly reminiscence
on skyrocketing egos and bar tabs,
hearts swerving between painted lines,
hiccups of raw talent like Indiana streetlamps
between swaths of the dark unknown.
Call it sophic delusion, cant or canto,
highways pulled taut as tin can telephones.
This is the melancholy men know:
brief triumph of the emptied shot glass,
heroism of late night boxing reruns,
hints of soured plans and disgruntled wives.
Then all at once, glancing up in time
to see some young, local beauty sashay in,
trailing stares and cheap perfume,
wearing her knotted handkerchief for a top.

How It Goes for Boys

In grade school, I'd spend the night
at Dustin's house. He had a water bed
and glow-in-the-dark stars on the ceiling.
He knew sports terminology
and had no interest in *Star Trek*.
He told me that one day
when he used to live in Arizona,
this girl across the courtyard
strolled naked onto her balcony
and waved at him. Such kindness,
such grace rippling that raw desert heat.
In high school, we started
hanging out less, afraid someone
would think we were gay, both of us
too shy to earn the favor
of Iowa daughters with Egyptian tans
and three rings through each ear.
We used to argue over religion,
his cherry-picked snips of Old Testament
versus my budding Zen and self-
doubt. Some nights, we'd climb a ladder
leaning against his dark roof
and unfurl our sleeping bags,
real stars crisping the country evening,
miles from motels and drive-thru's.
Nothing out there but cow pastures,
splintered fences, maybe a radio
with batteries duct-taped in the groove,
guitar solos and rap screeds

eventually dissolving into soft rock
as the moon kept slipping in
and out of her blue-black shawl.
And we slept, restless but free
of nightmares, always careful to leave
some untouched space between us.

Husband for a Day

Men would fuck retarded monkeys
if it were socially acceptable,
you say from the porch after work,

fireflies thick over the country lake.
Your friends perk up and nod,
snickering beneath Orion's

starry belt as they sip port
over the wild cricket-swells of night.
And I remember that lost

Sunday, your second husband gone.
You asked me to take you
to Lamaze class. So there I sat,

crotch in the small of your back,
ringed by pillows and pregnant women
breathing in choreographed gulps

while nervous men rubbed shoulders.
Relax—become your own inner peace
said the coach in a flowered leotard.

Suddenly, months of bloating
foghorned right out of you
in the true form of a grand tenuto fart,

reverberating over pan flutes
and votive candles, and you turned,
your face so red I fell in love.

Dust

It seems we've left skin
in each other's lungs. I should have

looked under your bed skirt
for my wallet, but how

could credit cards compare
to the sneeze after we've parted?

Gone and still you make me
reach for a tissue—still my palms

turn circles in the red
breakwater of your heartbeat.

I want to tell you, I have nothing
but respect for your ribcage

now that we both know
it's not big enough to hold us.

I Christen Thee, My Higgs Boson

Hardly has the wax seal dried
on this common twilight in late September
when I long for fingertips

I've never felt, reassurance
of starlings migrating over Wal-Mart,
calligraphy of the inexplicable

silence heard ever since I could talk
and asked what it was I saw,
just there on reality's platinum fringe.

No matter that men called it foolish,
that women smirked behind fans
and pronounced it sweet

for grown boys to be so lovesick,
this full of ache for what has no name,
lacking both mass and magic

but what, under a microscope,
under the dirty thumbnail of God,
could unstop all the laws of the universe.

For Tanya, Whose Fate Remains Unknown

The old woman who keeps calling me,
who leaves increasingly frantic voice mails
until she finally catches me climbing
the snowy steps to my apartment,
has bad news about my daughter, Tanya.

When I tell her I have no daughter,
she reads back my cell number as though
to ask if I meant that figuratively,
like Tanya could ever wrong me
enough that I'd revoke her surname.

The old woman's southern drawl
plays at double-rpm. I imagine Tanya
holding a bloody bath towel to one side,
her face frightfully pale as she tries
to recall her dad's work number.

What seeps between Tanya's fingers
if not memories of swim lessons,
of sweat that smelled like sauerkraut
as her father fussed in the guts of her car,
meticulously changing the fluids?

We humans have so few worthwhile
inventions—like vegetarianism,
whether you practice or not. Like driving
to where she lies, tethered to a drip
pole, quaking like a small animal.

But no, I say, I'm sorry, and forget
even to wish them luck before I hang up.
Outside, it starts to snow. My cat
mews and paws at the window, trying
to catch each flake before it melts.

Betting on the Wrong Horse

If a train moves southwest at eighty miles an hour
while another train moves northeast at half that speed,
and it's Tuesday, what's your favorite color?

I suppose I should tell you I think
sleep counts as a form of attempted suicide,
especially if dreams of hot air balloons

weaving through power lines are involved.
If you happen to be a fan of getting bitten
by snakes, you probably already know not to try

and suck out the poison, despite what Hollywood says.
I think this is important because at the moment,
I'm listening to Mozart so I can write

I'm listening to Mozart and maybe appear
a bit sultry and cultured, despite my pale background
of factory lines and hand-me-down

campers parked in the shadow of Iowa cedars.
On the day my mother died, I walked along the river
because I wanted to be alone, but didn't mind

when my uncle's Labrador padded after me—
the one killed by a pickup blaring Charlie Daniels
a summer or two later. The black Lab,

that is. Not my uncle, who still smokes
pot to stay sane for lack of therapy and pills.
Sometimes he walks along the same river

that ravels below abandoned train tracks,
looking for arrowheads washed up by the current.
He knows what is hidden never stays that way.

Dedication

In our house, not once did we hear
someone say *you're welcome*
in answer to thanks. Instead—*it's all right,*
backhanded reminder of the sacrifice
this or that Dollar Store trinket
cost folks well below the poverty line.
This is a hard habit to break.
Don't worry, it's fine when you thank me
for helping you move furniture
or coming to your reading,
your wedding, your beloved's funeral.
Oh, it's all right, to students
when they thank me for margin comments,
for letting them turn in assignments
half a semester late. *It's all right*—
the door held open a few seconds longer
for the jock on crutches,
for the blue-eyed girl breathing
into the straw fixed to her wheelchair.
I want to thank the moon for tilting
in time to highlight the rain
spilling off a parked windshield,
my body for keeping itself free
so far from cancer, diabetes, suicide.
I want to thank my fear of death
for melting whenever a beautiful woman
bends to drink from a fountain.
I want to thank the crows for mating
on any windowsill but mine.
And their answer, rising in chorus
with each day's rusty sunset:
It's all right. It's all right. It's all right.

Buying an Ice Scraper

Down past underwired mannequins,
aisles beyond the red tubes of buckshot
but before the Disney pacifiers,

I find them arrayed like minutemen—
midnight-blue, green as wormwood,
arm-length ones with bristles,

stubby ones sold two for ten bucks,
faces tipped like Japanese fans.
That easily, I am back in Osage, Iowa,

winter of my fourteenth year,
helping my brother scrape the ice
off the windshield of Dad's '77 Granada

with an empty Bon Jovi tape case,
wondering as I watched our breath rise
to curse the morning snowfall

gowning maples older than I was,
why life wasn't easier. Hundred below
with wind-chill, heater busted,

a sense already that in time
it could get worse. Later, as our father
withdrew the insulin needle

from our mother's blue forearm,
without turning, he asked us
why we hadn't looked under the seat.

Apologia

Those days when she found herself
banking on the alchemical grace
of a hemodialysis machine
that, quite literally, withdrew her lifeblood
a gulp at a time then routed it back,
freshly laundered, my brother and me
killed time at the coin shop down the street.
It did not seem strange to us,
that little hole-in-the-wall
where a war vet sold wheat pennies
for two cents, mint silver dollars
in clear plastic sleeves.
I recall a Mason jar of Buffalo Nickels
like the kind we'd sometimes
kick up on the river road,
faintly glinting in our footsteps.
The British fifty pence; the Hong Kong
two-dollar with its ruffled edges;
bright, two-tone pesos; and oddest of all
to farm boys with nothing to do,
Japanese coins with holes in the middle—
For string, the man said. *Just in case
you don't have pockets.* And it never entered
my mind to bring her back a necklace,
a kind of garish copper garland
she'd wear once she could walk again.
Once she was done trying
to laugh off the shock of being drained
down to her last drop of commerce,
never once asking us to stay.

Melancholia

After my mother's diabetes finally made me
half an orphan, my father and I drove north through
the white uppercuts of an Iowa snowstorm
to catch a plane to Fort Lauderdale,
then a cruise ship bound for the Bahamas.
My father saw the ad on late nite cable—
a day in Florida, plus two nights on the ocean.
All free, but not really. The boat rocked
like a drunken buoy, hefting shrimp scampi
from so many passengers that the crew tacked
barf-bags to the carpeted walls. No single women
under fifty, anyway. One afternoon, anchored
at the straw market in Nassau, honey-brown children
sold us Bob Marley tee-shirts made in Taiwan.
Then off to Blue Lagoon Island, a Caribbean speck
Hollywood forgot. A sign said they filmed
Gilligan's Island here, a few decades before broken
bottles and tourist shacks bled the place dry,
so that not even the ocean's raised skirts
could save us. I wandered like an astronaut
on bleach-tone sands, found my first native coconut,
read some D.H. Lawrence in a hammock
and spent the next twenty-four hours itching.
But at least this gave me a better reason
to turn down the kind advances of the gay
lookout, whose apparent job it was
to keep his eyes peeled for Caribbean icebergs.
I would like to end here by saying
some epiphany wriggled its way out of this,

maybe some analogy of death and consumerism
mitigated by me paying witness
to the enduring beauty of coconut trees,
or standing on the top-deck of that tin ship,
breathing—Whitmanesque—the moist night air
until I decided, in time, not to jump.
But I am not a liar, although I play one in real life.
I came home the same. My father remarried.
My mother, whom I love, is still dead.
Sometimes, when I write, I can feel myself
pushing a lawnmower over the space
where her body reaches, quietly, for the sky.

Climate Change

Maybe death is a party
so good, nobody wanders out for air.
But here, we bandy words
and paper in the weighty pause
between thunderheads.
During the day,
storms darken the sky.
At night, they brighten it.

The Basics

I was in fifth grade the day the nuns
brought in a nice Catholic doctor
to teach us about reproduction.

The boys, that is. A nurse arrived
to educate the girls while the doctor
herded the rest of us across the hall,

nervously told some jokes, chalked out
an absolutely sexless diagram
that omitted all the important parts.

We left more confused than before.
A few boys didn't even know the basics:
kind of like yours, but inside out,

my aunt said later, changing
her toddler-daughter's diaper while
I shifted balance in the doorway,

wanted to run outside and play
but knew, for the first time in my life,
I was learning something important.

In The Men's Locker Room at the YMCA

When the gray-haired man walks in
leading his daughter by the hand,
his daughter who looks to be three or four,
when he helps her undress for a shower,
both of them momentarily nude,
the father looking around to make sure
none of us are eyeing her too closely,
I look away. I am afraid
he would not understand my smile,
the pages of my memory turning back
to when I was her age, bathing
in the friendly shade of a woman
I knew by her breasts, her touch, her smile,
when I was small, never lonely,
and swollen with love for the world.

III

The Undirected Object

The Only Time a Woman Has Bought Me Flowers

I didn't know you could do that with food coloring. It was April. I was sixteen, working at a greasy spoon with Dustin, my best friend, when these two girls walked in. Two girls built like that S-curve that killed at least one carload of drunk kids each summer. They said they wanted to buy us roses, asked us what color. Dustin said yellow. I said blue. I'd read that there's no such thing as a blue rose, imagined them going to the florist and finding out I was so damn clever they'd just have to sleep with me. Only it turns out they just bought white roses and stuck them in vials with food coloring until the petals dyed, taped them to our car hoods and drove away, laughing. We walked through the windows, realizing for the first time that whatever magic women have, they always take it with them.

Ode to Dead Batteries

Still, it seems a bit ungrateful to just throw them away, after all the times they powered us through snow drifts, down highways when no one else would follow. The near-angelic glow they issued from our naked palms as we prowled backyards in our bathrobes, calling the name of some less faithful animal. Those insufferable evenings when we made them surf channels: past genocides, the ingratitude of solar panels, jaw-dropping footage of their long lost ancestor—the Baghdad Battery, circa 1 A.D., unearthed in Mesopotamia—and only our ignorance kept us from hearing their small voice cry *stop*. Sad mornings when they helped us wash last night's mistakes off our teeth. The Buddhists say that once you've rowed across the great river, why carry the row-boat with you? But I imagine all those batteries now: bagged with sewage, alone, though they never once mocked us for electric scissors, cameras to make amends for the frailty of our memories, and in beds all across our prairies and these broad, starry cityscapes, the hum of vibrators discretely, heroically filling in for Man's often less-than-miraculous touch.

Ode to a Flea Market Textbook

This one's yellowed pages insist we'll be living on the moon by 1977—same year Elvis died and I squirmed, a bit blue, from the hollows of a girl who heard from Hollywood that soon, we'd be orbiting Jupiter or gunning down cyborgs. Turns out writers have a lot in common with Jehovah's Witnesses: resetting their doomsday clocks, grumbling whenever the sun manages to soap-bubble out of the dark. And I think of that last haircut before a reconstruction surgery approved then canceled by Humana, certain that would be the last time I'd show half an ear to the world. Or the pretty girl I wanted to follow to her social work program in Manhattan, who turned out to be allergic to fidelity and something of a butterface once I got my eyes checked. Half-finished novels in the basement of my hard drive. All those American vows stored like crates in an airlock as I white-knuckle the flush valve, a bulimic astronaut yoked to that combusting gas ball we call practicality.

Between Tree and Ash

Between tree and ash: light—which is fire—which is hunger—which is *Why?*—which is mind—which is *wrong end of the telescope*—which is trumpet—which is swan—which is wolf—which is rifle—which is a wife waiting at home—which is worry, a yellow porch light—which is God before Tesla—which is astrology after stars—which is what you get for driving too fast—which is Rome—which was Carthage and Babylon—which was Zion—which was the cave murals of Lascaux, France: umber horses galloping over cliffs to avoid those stickmen with spears—which is us, minus desk lamps—which is the echo of rocks bashed until one threw a spark—which was sky—which was tree—which crackled then as now with God's hard-won applause.

God Minus One

A mishmash of Latin and Swahili, allusion to childhood's rim-rust sunsets, sweat-cloth of the union guy who yawned while driving his spear through the blue lattice of Christ's ribs—faith spelled backwards, juxtaposed with photos of bombed villages and the sorrow of Americans who look better with their clothes on. Air when nothing happens. The face-paint of Neanderthals, play of squirrels on a tombstone, *The Starry Night's* weight before it dried. This pull and push, difference between dark matter and dark energy. *Tangerine*—the color before the word. Why Maimonides hated foreskins. Why men cannot go too long without referencing the Nazis. Why comets hurtle like free-agent quarterbacks, adrenaline of the orgasm, childbirth in a universe full of black holes. Death not a period, but a comma. Stencils of that old equation, sopped up with biscuits and gravy—God, whatever she is, minus 1, plus x.

Girl Survives Sting from World's Most Venomous Creature

—AP Headline

Let's say you're a ten-year-old girl river-swimming in Queensland, Australia, in the summer heat of December—which is what happens when you live on the bottom-side of another hemisphere—when you get stung by a primordial blob that doubles as the deadliest thing since gunpowder, only something goes wrong (scientifically speaking) and you survive. What next? The lottery, the trapeze, conquering a bit of stage fright by standing in at the Sydney Opera House, maybe a tour in the local Special Forces with its seal of a sword-armed dragon? And when it finally comes—the inevitable heartbreak of human fallibility, so-and-so's lost battle with cancer or typhoid or whatever the hell else is out there, taut in the dark, waiting to strike—you can be the one who leans on the bedroom door like Achilles in a nightgown, maybe a slight smirk of wisdom. The one who waits for some quaking, hopeless creature you love to re-cradle the phone and cling to you the way the moon clings to the earth—the beautiful earth that knows enough to keep frailty at arm's length.

Hansel's Redemption

Years later, the witch burned and gone, the wilderness tamed, Hansel fell in love with his sister one night, watching how she undressed like some rare orchid beyond the chain lock of his hippocampus. For months afterward, he denied himself, taking extra hours at the saw mill so he could avoid seeing her flutter about the crumbling gingerbread house they'd inherited. This isn't real, he told himself. Just a misdirected echo from when we hugged naked in mother's oven, feeding off the dark. But each day it got stronger. Finally, he confessed. *I've always loved you, too,* she whispered over her third glass of blackberry wine. *Always.* Her Victoria's Secret nightgown fell like a discarded mask atop his workman's apron. We can't stay here, Hansel said. The villagers won't understand. So they made up new surnames, packed fishing rods and drove to Alaska, along the way necking at rest-stops like runaway sea horses. There's nothing wrong with this, Hansel promised. Love is love. Besides, we're not the first. I read somewhere that Egyptian pharaohs married their sisters to preserve the sanctity of the bloodline. *That doesn't sound very romantic,* Gretel said, and wiped the cold from his nose.

Miracle Mike

My backwater family named me after an archangel with stars for eyes and a rich tangle of solar flares for hair—the one who drove Lucifer right off the rim of Heaven—*not* that rooster from Fruita, Colorado who lived the better part of two years without his head. It's important that you understand.

This all started on a Monday. September 10th, 1945. The day after a million Japanese surrendered in China, but four days before a hurricane slapped blimps out of the skies of southern Florida. This—the rooster, not the hurricane—was seen by great throngs of circus folk, children in muddy overalls, tight-buttoned schoolmarms who thought it might be educational: puzzling over some bobbing flower with a brain stem, this feathered vegetable on yellow feet.

They say Mike—the rooster, not the archangel—took grain and water through an eyedropper positioned right over the nude, pink flaps of his esophagus. The farmer who took his head then took him on tour claims he found Mike sleeping with the remnants of his cranium tucked under one wing. The farmer figured something was wrong when he—the rooster, not the archangel—went on like a kind of poultry samurai, pecking with his neck-stump after everything went dark.

Call this *Phantom Head Syndrome,* if you like. At least something besides us—a feathered thing with too many claws—knew right from his gut that, real or not, what is felt must be protected.

After Watching ESPN Highlights

Since I can't be the heart and soul of the Pittsburgh Steelers, I will make it my goal henceforth to be the heart and soul of my favorite bar—although I must say, the competition is fierce. I am the rookie amidst veterans, cigar-smoking encyclopedias on foreign lagers and ales, shoulders slumped like linebackers in this black-lit haze.

Already I have been the regent of my half of the office, that pull-up bar I bought from the local drugstore, my freezer with its bouquets of frozen broccoli. People need goals. So here I am—downstaged by live jazz, swooning roughnecks waiting to be drafted, just another indentation in a fierce column of ruddy barstools.

Not a single article will be written on how our team overcame segregation. How our players struggle to transition from draft beer to something top shelf. Still, these are my people, my competition during this whole evening of stories and bad jokes, to decide whom we cannot live without.

Look—the cheerleading squad straining inside last year's uniforms, wondering how they got so tight. A few stools down: Mascara Incarnate with her fake I.D., wincing heroically over the throaty roundhouse of her gin and tonic. The bartender with his distinctly hands-off coaching style, his half-washed steins glinting like trophies.

Blue Collar Mothers

At day's end, uniforms sweat-stained the color of twilight, they head home from hours spent scrubbing toilets and flipping burgers—all those tasks for which rubber gloves are required. Only so many hours left for children who need scrubbing too, dinner and more dishes, husbands waiting to be thawed from the inside out. Then bed. Or, if there's time, lotion for hands that are losing their softness, their belief in the sanctity of aloe. The boss—always a kid fresh out of college. All his gestures end in bleach, meat, wrinkled bags spilling out of the freezer. More gloves arrive, this time in two different colors: clear and turquoise. *This is America,* he says. *You ladies can choose.*

The History of Socialism

Socialism was invented in the 1960s by a wayward glass-blower named Karl Marx. Many historians cite the un-American way he said nothing about America. His wife, who invented tie-dye and same-sex marriage, initially supported him but later sued on behalf of Jesus Christ for plagiarism. Socialism differs from other forms of governance in that it encourages people to go outside. Other notable socialists: Achilles, Saint Augustine, and Darth Vader. The basic premise of socialism requires the mass import of Canadian hemp in exchange for lower gas prices. A socialist economy relies on bartering—say, one healthy donkey for a heart transplant. According to celebrated paleontologist, Dr. James Dobson, the socialists' chief symbol—the apple, *Malus domestica*, cousin of the white rose—could not have existed in the Garden of Eden since Turkey is nowhere near Texas. He further suggests that climate change might be responsible for apple seeds resembling the Star of David. It should be noted that even socialists disagree over which came first: the rooster or the scalpel, the rose or the holy worm.

Bad Similes

Please—not one more line stating how things look, smell, or taste *like sex*. As though this were the universal solvent of the figurative world, implying a single common denominator to get the audience nodding. But we know, or should, how absurd we look flapping away at each other, yet strangely how graceful a few seem doing it on film; how musk is like a fingerprint that changes depending on the day, the hour; that the taste is sometimes like water poured from a seashell, other times like a strong White Russian drunk from the cupped hands of a girl who was just handling pennies. As for the shape—the flesh-hinge that squeaks despite its freshly oiled gears, that time-lapse fumble of origami, that bit of runaway hydraulics hell-bent on blowing itself skyward.

IV

Divine Prepositions

Upon Hearing There Are At Least
300 Sextillion Stars in the Universe

A strange coincidence, they're calling it.
That many fireballs parading past our lenses,
wheeling through our biblical equations.
Not the sum of all the sand grains on a beach—
no, more like all the cells in all the bodies
of all the human beings on earth.
Just a coincidence. Strange.
The notion that we are all just threads
in a spangled sackcloth, clothed electrons
circling a yellow mitochondria,
single-minded glyphs of hemoglobin
rushing through the bloodstream of God.
No wonder we cannot see Her face
without going mad. How to go back
to folding slacks and tooling an engine?
Even our fascists are phagocytes,
even bums are six-winged macrophages.
Our gluons roil like cherubim. Breathe,
and you'll outrun the stars you prayed to.

American Malaise

I am trying to enjoy the Winter Olympics.
It's hard. I don't even like hockey
during odd-numbered years,
let alone now when all the players
have names I can't pronounce.
And speed skating—so tough to care
about a stranger blurring past
those popping flashbulbs, triumph or tragedy
of careers I've never cared to follow.
Even the grace of that Slovakian girl
mixing skiing with rifle practice
cannot hold my attention.
Still, all this pomp and circumstance
has me feeling guilty. To me,
the Olympics are like the United Nations.
Sure, it's an odd, mishandled mess,
but aren't we better off,
enriched somehow by the idea?
Maybe they should make us wait longer,
think of the Olympics like a comet
you're lucky to see once,
let alone thirty-odd times in one lifespan.
But there are so many of us now
crowding the planet, itching for glory.
Far be it for me to deny athletes
their pedestal, their laurel crown,
their little disk of metal
drawn out of the same soil we must
all one day rest in, decay washing over us:
the world's oldest form of applause.

State of the Union I

I'm starting to wonder if this is a trend
when another kid from a poetry class
shoots up his private corner of the universe,
this time a Congressional meet-and-greet
in front of a Safeway supermarket,
more names added to the roster
of In-the-Wrong-Place-at-the-Wrong-Time,
more American bystanders snuffed out
by the business end of free verse.
Sure, the best writing classes are asylums
for the metaphysically strained,
but now handguns come with clips
that hold thirty bad ideas—
exactly twenty-nine more than those
owned by the powdered madmen
who drafted the Second Amendment.
But I am thirty-two now (older than Oswald,
younger than Christ) and tired of arguing
with myself, knowing that none
of my poems could pass a background check.
Today, I shoulder into each classroom
and scan the rows of aspiring poets
for hints that I should trade my sport coat
for something in Kevlar. So far,
I've lucked out. Meaning if my luck changes,
this poem will be especially ironic.
Maybe said irony will help it go viral.
The first poem printed in *The Economist*,
recited by Wolf Blitzer's bumbling monotone
on CNN, grieving families tuning in

to the thought of classrooms
not as war zones or retroactive pagodas,
but trauma wards in mankind's oldest hospital—
which of course they aren't. Until they are.

State of the Union II

I dreamt that someone—maybe you—assigned my poems
to your class. And I happened to be in the hallway

when one student stopped you outside your office to ask
if you were done with me, would be all right if she sold

me back to the bookstore now, even though it's still
ten weeks before summer. And you smiled, understanding

that for the price of my odes to repairmen and snowmelt,
she could get a latté three days in a row, maybe buy

that album her boyfriend—who says poetry is gay—
wants for Valentine's Day. An album she doesn't care for

but he'll leave it playing while they undress each other
in her dorm room, her roommate off studying French,

a votive candle burning on her pressboard desk
in defiance of residence hall policy. And because of how

she heard those songs, and when, even years later
when they come on in a shopping mall while she pushes

a baby stroller next to her dissatisfied mate, she'll stop,
oddly quiet, and turn to hide the wetness in her eyes.

Affirmative Action

When the black woman walks in
with her child, I think about giving up
the best seat in the coffee shop,
which happens to be my seat,
way in the back by the big window
overlooking a patch of lawn,
bees hauling their fondness
for the tulips planted along the curb,
because yes, isn't it awful—
that whole slavery thing
we learned about in textbooks,
and shouldn't we show her
how different we are, you and me
with our tornado bait ancestors
and our manicured haircuts?
The black mother turns to go,
toddler on her skirts, as though both see
the danger of lingering too long
in the sweet mist of espresso,
of stopping to read the newspaper
while wreathed by our familiar smiles,
our strained, toothy kindness.

No Young Man's Craft

Good, but maybe not so good
as he thinks he is, says the retired professor
sipping merlot at the Fickle Peach
in answer to Rob's query,
set to the dull smack of billiards:
So, how good a poet is my little brother?

To prove him right, I wander free
of Yeats' *Sailing to Byzantium,*
which this Greek-bearded professor quotes
rhyme on rhyme from memory,
my ears slack, my eyes drawn more
to the doggerel of a passing cleavage line.

Then for no reason, I start to think
about the Tibetan singing bowl I bought,
how I tried to write about it
but spelled *bowel* instead of *bowl,*
so days later, I still smile at the thought.
My little place alive with the hum

of Tibetan bowels—great ones
shaped from hand-hammered bronze.
Mine come from Nepal and weigh 188 grams.
On the inside of my bowels,
someone wrote *om mani padme hum.*
Cherry blossoms wreath the outer rim.

With the help of a mallet, my bowels
produce multiphonic and polyharmonic overtones.
My bowels also came with a free cushion,
kind of beige with golden trim,
and were designed to align my Chakras
by emitting a steady C note.

According to customer reviews,
my bowels possess *antique charm, good sheen,*
and *a gentle, mellowing spirit.*
They can also be rung like gongs
with the aid of a wool-wrapped striker.
But this requires almost no skill.

Mother's Day

Now that my mother is dead, I'm free
the second Sunday of my every May

to go fishing, to not call home,
to run around the yard with scissors.

I can shy away from Hallmark stores
and not feel guilty for going out

with unwashed ears. If I like, later,
I'll splurge on wine and a nice dinner—

alone, of course, since all my friends
are off with their smiling makers,

presenting boxed gratitude in a house
whose door they close behind them.

Turritopsis Nutricula

Turns out it's not so hard to live forever.
All you have to do is be a jellyfish—

turritopsis nutricula, to be precise.
True, it would be tough to drive a car

or climb trees as a translucent bell
of four or five millimeters, bobbing along

in tropical oceans, hitchhiking
in the ballasts and hulls of cruise ships.

But there's much to be said for being
able to age in reverse, to shed

your own tentacles at each new rebirth.
To go on, even if it means forgetting

all those miles of sea, the sun eclipsed
whenever whales swam overhead.

Lessons of the Linothorax

The Greek hoplites made their armor
out of linen glued layer on layer
with a tough leather core,

stiff at first, until body heat
made it mold to the wearer's torso,
each one like a battle-worn fingerprint.

They say it was easy to repair,
kneeling in some fourth world ditch—
just peel back the torn layer,

glue on a new one. But what if
some poor bastard took a bronze blade
straight down to the heart,

that shy, flightless cardinal?
Fields torched, supplies run short.
Now you are the one fingering

the slice of a Persian spear
that left you minus one buddy.
There you kneel with thread and paste,

dogs and crows waiting already,
waiting in the wings. How to ignore
your new armor's scar, how the cold strata

of a dead man's ribcage
reshapes itself to embrace you?
How not to pause over your whetstone

just as the sun crests Marathon
and think there must be a lesson here—
that one day, men will learn it?

Leda's Response

Well, for one thing,
he was hung like a swan.
That aside, I've grown
sick of healing. Sick
of telling the same story
to biographers,
being typecast
by English majors
who have never even
been overseas.
I know how the sun
slants through olive trees;
how water lilies move,
move, stop moving.
We are none of us
born to be metaphors.

Persephone and Oedipus

Tired of arguing over who wears the sadder fate,
Persephone and Oedipus decide to get drunk.

Oedipus knows this little Irish pub down the street,
a basement place with rusty swords on the wall.

He buys the first round, sips his Johnny Walker Black
and hopes she doesn't catch his wince. But

Persephone is too busy wondering if her filmy gown
is the wrong attire for this place, her nipples

swaying like figs at the end of the bartender's stare.
I'm tired of being a metaphor, Oedipus grumbles,

clenching his bruised knuckles around his shotglass.
Persephone nods, spine arched like a scimitar.

He stares at her then asks, *Want to do some blow?*
She says yes, but only if they go to the ladies' room.

It's cleaner in there, she says. Oedipus frowns.
I thought you said you've never been here before!

Persephone readjusts her gown. *I haven't*, she said,
but everywhere you go, it's the same damn story.

Parable

On the morning of the great battle,
the knights woke in such a fuss
that they dressed themselves backwards—
metal first, then cloth, then flesh
and last of all, their organs, hung like
ripe apples from the war-tree.

Well, this is embarrassing, they said,
then saw their enemies had done likewise.
How to fight once you've seen
the contents of your foe's stomach,
the sad obstructions around his heart?

Peace spread across Europe
which led to boredom, which led
to war. Except the men's sons rebelled
and wore their armor on the outside.

Their fathers gathered on the road
to watch them ride off. The old men's tears
rusted their insides. Outside,
though, they still looked
as always like they were blushing.

Augurs and Haruspices

I wonder if they got along way back in post-Etruscan Rome
when all hinged on omens. Scrabbling with the livers of sheep,

noting the chatter and flight of birds—one stroking a ready
knife, friendly with every butcher; the other convinced the gods

fine-tuned each chirping syllable. Did the augurs gloat when
no haruspex handed Pope Innocent easy victory over the Visigoths?

Or were they too busy noting the pecking habits of starved
chickens, patterns in the dust? Perhaps they were like painters

and poets, carpenters and bricklayers, debtors and thieves.
At day's end, they meet in an Aventine tavern. A few prattle on

about birds seen by Romulus himself while others roll
their bloodshot eyes, forks straining prophecy from their stew.

Then Again

It makes sense—Pilate, constipated,
consigned to a realm of muck and sand,
a dead child or two named after dead forebears
preserved in the dying flower
of his own brain, when suddenly—
the very Son of God, the Messiah himself,
shuffles into the afternoon's affairs,
but all the fool can do is stare
and offer up aristocratic mumblings
on the need to give up what he's never had.

Think of what you would do
if the son of the boss who made you work
through your daughter's birthday
showed up and said it was your fault.
If the landlord who left you
bankrupt sent someone to announce
tough shit, you're still a loser,
but kiss my ass a little more and we'll see.
Or, at best, *maybe I was wrong*
but hey, no guarantees on tomorrow.

How not to give the centurions the nod?
How not to do unto the son of Caesar
as Caesar has done unto you?
Sorry, kid, says everyman Pilate.
Come back when you have a better deal.
And Christ understands, having grown up
in halls painted with ram's blood,
the first black lamb of his flock
to wipe red palms on his mother's gown
and embrace the gene for mercy.

Zen for Dummies

In the campus courtyard,
two girls with Greek on their sweaters
talk shop—boys, hangovers,
stylists, then at last,
the assigned pages from
a fat tome on world religions,
lying like an open fist
on the wrapper-strewn grass
before them. Both confess failing
that last quiz over Islam.
I catch the word *Zen*
before one asks what the book means
by *emptiness*. The other
tugs her hot-pink bra strap, says:
That life is meaningless—
but, you know, in a good way.

From One Poet to Another

It was only a matter of time
before one of us mentioned Icarus.
Or Christ. Or Hitler.
Then compared the heart
to a pomegranate seed
tilled from the well of a ribcage
while, elsewhere, something happened
that involved cicadas.
No one cares to hear anymore
about your mother, that recurring dream
about elephants with skyscraper legs
crossing a Dalí landscape.
How you really *get* Miles Davis.
The sun, that yellow bat,
left us stranded at light's length.
So here: two mossy stones,
two thimbles of rain.
We will cross this waste together.

Sunday Afternoon at the Books-A-Million

The boy in the oversized fleece
hanging halfway down his train rail arms
moves through the bookstore
with Beyoncé
blasting out of his pocket.

No headphones. He struts past
discount tables heaped with Sarah Palin,
past a book of knots
that shows pictures of knots
but not how to make them.

Then he finds her—his girlfriend
with her pink purse
and infected lip ring.

See how hard they try
not to grin as they hurry past
aisle after aisle of Christian fan fiction,
a lone rack of sex guides,
calendars of dragons in repose.

The boy says something
the girl likes. She laughs. They shark
through a sea of baby strollers.

Soon, they will leave us
with our manuals on faucet repair,
our harlequin theories on economics,
our paintings of tortured saints
gazing wetly at the sky.

This is not good news. We should mourn.
For these two, surely the great
glass doors will open wide.

Poem in Which I, and Only I, Get What I Deserve

A student with manga-blue eyes
submits a poem about her father's hands
and their ability, when closed,

to chip more than teeth. I remember
four years of boxing lessons,
the reason I stayed late

and pressed iron bars against the ceiling,
the nunchakus I practiced
to the trill of imaginary pan flutes

after another female friend told me
of what so-and-so had done
and I shuddered from the weight of it all.

I give her the number for counseling.
Then, in a poor attempt
to lighten the mood, ask her

if she wants me to go kick his ass.
She looks me up and down.
Says: *I'm pretty sure he could take you.*

Last Poem of the Day

You rise at three-thirty in the morning
just as I'm giving up on a sonnet, the pieces
scattered like whale bones amid tousled
pages from history books and one
from a dictionary dog-eared for *rubenesque*—
salmonberry nightgown loosely tied,
you kiss me then barefoot to the
bathroom,
slump half-asleep while you urinate,
the faint tinkling drowning out the grand-
father clock ticking in the dark study,
your gown slack enough to reveal
between noun and verb the pink comma
of your nipple, and my heart swells
right before you frown and close the door.

Number Twenty-Five

Let's hear it for Charles W. Campbell,
a one-time carpenter from Iowa
(late of Custer's 7th Cavalry, G Company)
who joined a squad fetching water
to wet the lips of the dying wounded
when he took a rifle slug to the shoulder,
told the rest to go on without him
and missed his shot at a Medal of Honor.
Gallantry in action, they called it.
Twenty-four awarded to boys carrying jugs
of dirty river to the mouths
of other boys who got themselves
mangled up and gut-shot by the natives,
a storm of Lakota and Cheyenne
with good rifles and nothing to lose.
Historians go silent after this—
at least so far as Campbell is concerned.
Maybe he went back to driving nails
with his good arm, showing off
that knotty scar to flouncing barmaids.
Until one day, he finds his fists
the color of liver-stained sackcloth,
steadying the ladder his grandson climbs.
It's autumn. The roof needs mending.
The grandson skips over loose sheathing.
He is tired of being scolded.
So young, he cannot imagine falling
into that wide, fretful embrace.

Ode to Steve-O

Maybe a TV show called *Jackass*
doesn't belong in these hallowed halls
next to Basho and Yeats,

Whitman shaking his white locks
enough to warp a runaway sun,
but let me plead this one exception:

this stuntman with his own face
tattooed on his back, life-size portraiture
gracing his flagpole spine—

eye to mouth, brow to thumbs-up.
Surely what today we call silly
will grow into nostalgia, then tragedy

as age wrinkles our wild grins,
unravels our ability to clean ourselves
of each cells' indigestible waste.

This is what happens with age:
the past becomes a myth, a tattoo
we haul behind us but can't quite see.

After a Promising Student
Besmirched D.H. Lawrence

It's hard to appreciate lions
after you've seen how they kill elephants,
a pack of toothy orphans
piling on the back of the king,
the king who leaves them
with plenty, the lions gnawing
and gnawing like bratty ticks until he falls,
then strutting afterward
with blood on their snouts, strutting
like it takes guts to kill
what can't turn its head to bite you,
what could have trampled you
to porridge but didn't—what showed
no contempt for your young,
only wanted to be left alone
so it could rest from all this heat,
tusks down, and cool itself
by drinking its own reflection.

After Reading That 99.999…%
of an Atom Is Empty Space

The more we prod the stuff of substance,
dry gaps between flecks of protons,
the more we find nothing here but unused lots.

Still, skyscrapers sway. Infants crawl.
Men stub their toes on coffee tables then fire
whomever did what in the copy room.

Missiles arc over Jerusalem—oddly
hollow, oddly not—then something dissolves
that couldn't be proven to exist, anyway.

See here: more bones of pirated stardust.
Even touch is the absence of contact.
Even God is the absence of God.

Carpe Diem, Quam Minimum Credula Postero

The pretty young writer I meet for coffee
asks me if I think she needs to grow up.

I tell her *No, you have an old soul,* and we laugh
at the thought of her soul dying before

her body, like maturity or wisdom
or whatever the hell you want to call it

whittles away years in the having,
like enlightenment is just a house guest

who shows up and starts charging you rent.
As I'm leaving, a friend calls. Someone

we went to grad school with just died—
another warning shot fired across the bow

of our mortality, another one who shared
our halls and air gone from a hiccup in the brain,

an arterial comma splice you pay for
with all the empathy of an overdraft fee,

a late fine at the video store which turns out
to be everything you have, all the grace

you squirreled away, down to that last
holy shilling. This is the debt we owe

for what does not but should leave us
breathless, present, speaking in tongues.

Acknowledgements

322 Review – "Damnatio Memoriae"

African American Review – "Affirmative Action," "Why Girls Walk Home"

American Poetry Journal – "Post Grads"

Anti-Poetry – "Number Twenty-Five"

Another Chicago Magazine – "From One Poet to Another," "Poem in Which I, and Only I, Get What I Deserve"

Atticus Books Poetry Break – "Persephone and Oedipus"

caesura – "Hansel's Redemption"

Guernica – "Dust"

Hayden's Ferry – "Ode to the Boxing Clapboard"

Juked – "The World's Oldest Dildo"

Los Angeles Review – "The Birthdays of Ex-Lovers"

Mandala – "Zen for Dummies"

Mid-American Review – "Ode to Dead Batteries"

New York Quarterly – "Mother's Day," "To the President of the American Begonia Society"

Pearl – "Husband for a Day"

Poetry Quarterly – "In the Men's Locker Room at the YMCA," "Ode to Coprolite," "Then Again"

Prime Mincer – "Dear Brigitte Nielsen"

Rattle – "Dedication"

Re)verb – "Before Rilke was a Man," "Last Poem of the Day"

Rosebud – "Skandha"

Strange Horizons – "I Christen Thee, My Higgs Boson"

"Ode to Dead Batteries" was a finalist for the Fineline Competition.

"Skandha" was reprinted on *Verse Daily*.

Some of these poems also appeared in *Pure Elysium,* a limited edition chapbook which won the Palettes and Quills 2nd Biennial Chapbook Contest.

About the Author

Michael Meyerhofer grew up in Iowa where he learned the value of reading pulp novels, lifting weights, and not getting his hopes up. He attended the University of Iowa before receiving his M.F.A. from Southern Illinois University, Carbondale. He currently lives in Indiana where he teaches poetry, collects medieval weapons, and stays up late, writing politically charged letters to the editor. He also just recently published *Wytchfire*, a literary fantasy novel and (hopefully) the first in a series.

Michael Meyerhofer's third book, *Damnatio Memoriae*, won the Brick Road Poetry Book Contest. His previous books are *Blue Collar Eulogies* (Steel Toe Books) and *Leaving Iowa* (winner of the Liam Rector First Book Award). He has also won five chapbook prizes. His work has appeared in *Ploughshares*, *North American Review*, *Arts & Letters*, *River Styx*, *Quick Fiction* and other journals, and can be read online at www.troublewithhammers.com.

Our Mission

The mission of Brick Road Poetry Press is to publish and promote poetry that entertains, amuses, edifies, and surprises a wide audience of appreciative readers. We are not qualified to judge who deserves to be published, so we concentrate on publishing what we enjoy. Our preference is for poetry geared toward dramatizing the human experience in a language rich with sensory image and metaphor, recognizing that poetry can be, at one and the same time, both familiar as the perspiration of daily labor and outrageous as a carnival sideshow.

Also Available from Brick Road Poetry Press

www.brickroadpoetrypress.com

Dancing on the Rim by Clela Reed

Possible Crocodiles by Barry Marks

Pain Diary by Joseph D. Reich

Otherness by M. Ayodele Heath

Drunken Robins by David Oates

Lotus Buffet by Rupert Fike

The Melancholy MBA by Richard Donnelly

Two-Star General by Grey Held

Chosen by Toni Thomas

Etch and Blur by Jamie Thomas

BRICK ROAD
POETRY PRESS

About the Prize

The Brick Road Poetry Prize, established in 2010, is awarded annually for the best book-length poetry manuscript. Entries are accepted August 1st through November 1st. The winner receives $1000 and publication. For details on our preferences and the complete submission guidelines, please visit our website at www.brickroadpoetrypress.com.